HEALTH HELPERS

I NEED A THERAPIST

By Rachel Rose

Consultant: Beth Gambro
Reading Specialist, Yorkville, Illinois

BEARPORT
PUBLISHING

Minneapolis, Minnesota

Teaching Tips

Before Reading

- Look at the cover of the book. Discuss the picture and the title.

- Ask readers to brainstorm a list of what they already know about therapists. What can they expect to see in the book?

- Go on a picture walk, looking through the pictures to discuss vocabulary and make predictions about the text.

During Reading

- Read for purpose. Encourage readers to think about the kinds of things that someone might see a therapist for.

- Ask readers to look for the details of the book. How can a therapist help?

- If readers encounter an unknown word, ask them to look at the sounds in the word. Then, ask them to look at the rest of the page. Are there any clues to help them understand?

After Reading

- Encourage readers to pick a buddy and reread the book together.

- Ask readers to name two things they might find at a therapist's office. Find the pages that tell about these things.

- Ask readers to write or draw something they learned about therapists as health helpers.

Credits

Cover and title page, © LIGHTFIELD STUDIOS/Adobe Stock and © irina88w/iStock; 3, © LightFieldStudios/iStock; 5, © Deepak Sethi/iStock; 7, © StefaNikolic/iStock; 8–9, © aquaArts studio/iStock; 10–11, © Prostock-studio/Shutterstock; 13, © zilvergolf/Adobe Stock; 15, © monkeybusinessimages/iStock; 16–17, © Synthetic-Exposition/iStock; 19, © Ridofranz/iStock; 21, © Phynart Studio/iStock; 22TL, © John_Kasawa/iStock; 22TR, © i_tkach/Adobe Stock, © New Africa/Adobe Stock, and © New Africa/Adobe Stock; 22MR, © MicroStockHub/iStock; 22BL, © Nenov/iStock; 22BR, © t_kimura/iStock; 23TL, © PhotoMelon/iStock; 23TR, © skynesher/iStock; 23BL, © kool99/iStock; 23BR, © SDI Productions/iStock.

See BearportPublishing.com for our statement on Generative AI Usage.

Library of Congress Cataloging-in-Publication Data

Names: Rose, Rachel, 1968- author.
Title: I need a therapist / by Rachel Rose.
Description: Minneapolis, Minnesota : Bearport Publishing Company, [2025] |
   Series: Health helpers | Includes bibliographical references and index.
Identifiers: LCCN 2024021914 (print) | LCCN 2024021915 (ebook) | ISBN
   9798892326353 (library binding) | ISBN 9798892327152 (paperback) | ISBN
   9798892326759 (ebook)
Subjects: LCSH: Psychotherapists--Juvenile literature. |
   Psychotherapy--Juvenile literature.
Classification: LCC RC480 .R664 2025 (print) | LCC RC480 (ebook) | DDC
   616.89/14--dc23/eng/20240621
LC record available at https://lccn.loc.gov/2024021914
LC ebook record available at https://lccn.loc.gov/2024021915

Copyright © 2025 Bearport Publishing Company. All rights reserved. No part of this publication may be reproduced in whole or in part, stored in any retrieval system, or transmitted in any form or by any means, electronic, mechanical, photocopying, recording, or otherwise, without written permission from the publisher.

For more information, write to Bearport Publishing, 5357 Penn Avenue South, Minneapolis, MN 55419.

Contents

A Therapist Helps 4

Therapist Tools 22

Glossary 23

Index 24

Read More 24

Learn More Online 24

About the Author 24

A Therapist Helps

My best friend is moving.

I feel very sad.

Who can help me?

I need a **therapist**!

Say therapist like
THER-uh-pist

A lot of people want to talk to the therapist.

The therapist is very busy.

I have to wait.

Then, it is my turn.

My therapist and I sit at a small table.

There are toys.

They say I can play while we talk.

I pick the sand!

I feel **shy**.

My therapist gives me a big smile.

They ask me what I like to do.

I tell them about myself.

My therapist is kind.

So, I tell them why I am sad.

My best friend is leaving.

I start to cry.

I have so many big feelings.

My therapist says it is okay to cry.

Everyone feels sad sometimes.

I talk about my **emotions**.

Sometimes, they make it hard to do things.

My therapist listens.

It feels good to talk.

The therapist gives me paper and **crayons**.

I draw a picture for my friend.

This helps me share my feelings.

I finish my drawing.

It is time to go home.

I feel much better.

Thanks, therapist!

Therapist Tools

A therapist uses many tools.

- A table
- Pictures
- A toy
- Crayons
- Paper

Glossary

crayons colored wax for drawing

emotions feelings

shy feeling a little scared

therapist a person who helps with feelings

Index

emotions 16
friend 4, 12, 18
listen 16
sad 4, 12, 14
sand 8
talk 6, 8, 16
toys 8

Read More

Chang, Kirsten. *Sad (Blastoff! Readers: Emotions).* Minneapolis: Bellwether Media, Inc., 2025.

Hughes, Sloane. *Don't Sweat It: How to Navigate Big Emotions (Life Works!).* Minneapolis: Bearport Publishing Company, 2022.

Learn More Online

1. Go to **FactSurfer.com** or scan the QR code below.
2. Enter "**Need Therapist**" into the search box.
3. Click on the cover of this book to see a list of websites.

About the Author

Rachel Rose is a life coach. Like a therapist, she helps people feel better by talking about their feelings.